# Riches from Nature

by Margie Burton, Cathy French and Tammy Jones

## Table of Contents

My mom and dad say that
if I help take care of the earth,
the earth will help take care of me.

# How Do We Use What Is Inside the Earth?

Sometimes, I dig down inside the earth
to see what is there.

I see a lot of rocks inside the earth.

There are rocks
inside the earth.

My mom says that some people
find gold inside the earth.

There is gold
inside the earth.

My mom tells me that we get oil and gas from deep inside the earth.

This oil pump is taking the oil out of the earth.

She says that we use the oil and gas
in many ways.

We use gas to make our car go.

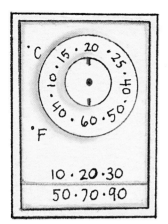

We can use oil and gas for heat.

We can use oil and gas to make things work around our house.

My dad says that we must not use up all of the things that we get from inside the earth because we cannot make these things again.

# How Do We Use What Is On the Earth?

When I look around, I see things
on the earth, too. I see soil
on the earth. My mom and dad and I use
the soil on the earth to grow plants for food.

My dad tells me that the bricks
on our house are made from a kind of soil, too.

He is using bricks to make a wall.

When I look
around, I see trees
on the earth.

My mom says that
the trees give us paper.
The paper for this book
was made from a tree.

Trees give us wood, too.
My dad uses the wood from
trees to heat our home.

When I look around, I can see
water on the earth.

My mom says
we need water
to drink. We cannot
live without it.

We also eat some of the
things that live in the water.

When I look around, I see animals on the earth. Animals help give us food.

Animals also help give us clothes.

The sheep's wool
is used to make this sweater.

## How Do We Use What Is Above the Earth?

Air is above the earth. I cannot see the air, but my dad says that it is there. He says that we need air to live.

I can see the sun above the earth.
We need the sun to help keep us warm.

Solar panels keep this house warm
by using heat from the sun.

I think my mom and dad are right.
If I help take care of the earth,
the earth will help take care of me!